DNA

Wendy Conklin, M.A.

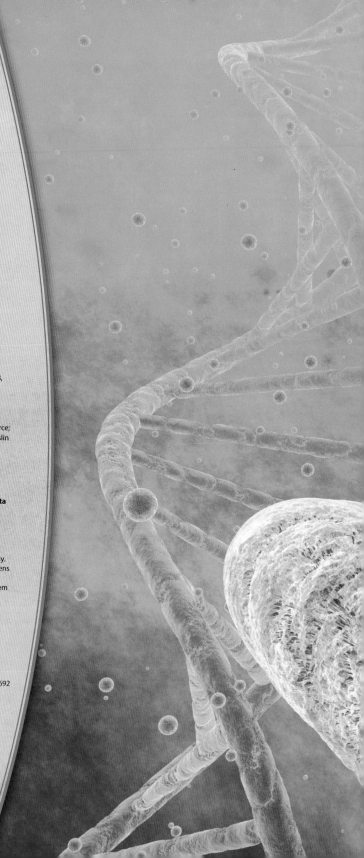

Consultant

Jill Tobin
California Teacher of the Year
Semi-Finalist
Burbank Unified School District

Publishing Credits

Rachelle Cracchiolo, M.S.Ed., *Publisher*
Conni Medina, M.A.Ed., *Managing Editor*
Diana Kenney, M.A.Ed., NBCT, *Content Director*
Dona Herweck Rice, *Series Developer*
Robin Erickson, *Multimedia Designer*
Timothy Bradley, *Illustrator*

Image Credits: Cover, pp.1, 14, 21, 31 iStock; pp.6-8, 20 Science Source, p.7 Science Photo Library; p.10 Science Picture Co/Science Source; pp.12, 18, 23-25 Alamy; p.16 Getty Images; p.17 (top) iStock, (bottom) Scott Camazine/Science Source; p.20 (top) Laguna Design/Science Source; p.21 3D4Medical/Science Source; p.23 (top) Bill Sanderson/Science Source, (bottom) Roslin Institute/Newscom; p. 24 UPI/Newscom; p. 25 James King-Holmes/Science Source; pp. 28-29 (illustrations) Timothy Bradley; all other images from Shutterstock.

Library of Congress Cataloging-in-Publication Data

Conklin, Wendy, author.
  DNA / Wendy Conklin, M.A.
    pages cm
  Summary: "Twins can look identical. And siblings or children may look similar to other people in their family. Even kittens can have the same markings as other kittens in a litter. But why? The answer is DNA. DNA is what makes family members look similar but also makes them unique. DNA is what makes you, well, you!"-- Provided by publisher.
  Audience: Grades 4-6.
  Includes index.
  ISBN 978-1-4807-4719-7 (pbk.)
  1. DNA--Juvenile literature.
  2. Genes--Juvenile literature. I. Title.
  QP624.C65 2016
  572.8'6--dc23
                                        2015002692

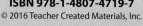

Teacher Created Materials
5301 Oceanus Drive
Huntington Beach, CA 92649-1030
http://www.tcmpub.com
ISBN 978-1-4807-4719-7
© 2016 Teacher Created Materials, Inc.

Table of Contents

Blueprint for Life

Does everyone in your family have the same big ears? Have you ever wondered why you have the same nose as your Aunt Alice? You probably have physical characteristics that are similar to some of your family members. Perhaps people have even told you that you look "exactly" like your brother. Well, unless you have an identical twin brother, that isn't really true. Each of us is unique because of a teeny-tiny but very important thing called *DNA*.

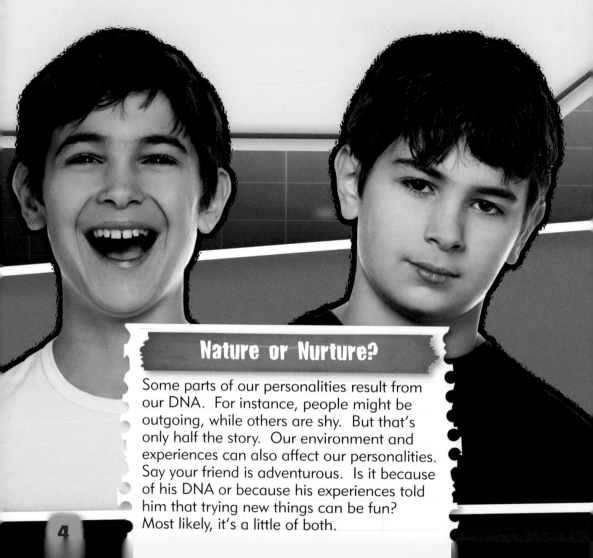

Nature or Nurture?

Some parts of our personalities result from our DNA. For instance, people might be outgoing, while others are shy. But that's only half the story. Our environment and experiences can also affect our personalities. Say your friend is adventurous. Is it because of his DNA or because his experiences told him that trying new things can be fun? Most likely, it's a little of both.

Twintastic

Identical twins are the only people who can have the same DNA. They start as one cell that divides to form two identical babies.

DNA is short for **deoxyribonucleic** (dee-OK-si-rahy-boh-NOO-klee-ik) **acid**. This is a key ingredient for life on Earth. Cells use the information found in DNA to grow, reproduce, and more. Cells are the building blocks of all life, including plants, animals, and people. Cells make up your entire body. This includes your eyelashes, earlobes, fingernails, heart, and everything that makes you *you*. In fact, your body has trillions of cells. And DNA acts as the "boss" of these cells.

DNA tells cells how to build a person. It instructs some cells how to become skin and tells other cells how to become blood. DNA tells each part of your body what its function is. Everything your body does happens because of DNA.

Understanding DNA

To really understand how DNA works, we must first understand cells. Even though they are very small, cells come in many shapes and sizes, and they do different things. Some organisms have trillions of cells, while other organisms have only one cell. Regardless of these differences, cells share a basic structure. All cells contain ribosomes that make proteins. Every cell contains mitochondria (mahy-tuh-KON-dree-uh), which are powerhouses that turn food into energy.

More advanced cells have a nucleus. The nucleus serves as the control center, or brain, for the cell. It communicates with the cell, telling it what to do, where to go, and how it should look. Tiny strands of DNA are found packed inside the nucleus. Each piece of DNA is made of a long chain of molecules. If you were to stretch out a tiny strand, it would measure about 3 meters (10 feet) long! In fact, if you were able to stretch out all of your DNA, it would be a very thin line, but it would stretch nearly 16 billion kilometers (10 billion miles)—twice the distance to Pluto! And it's all packed in the nucleus of your cells.

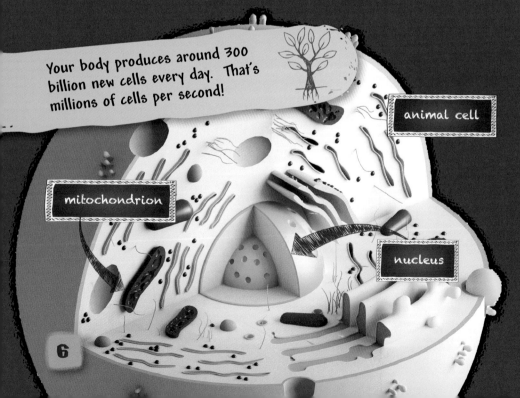

Your body produces around 300 billion new cells every day. That's millions of cells per second!

animal cell

mitochondrion

nucleus

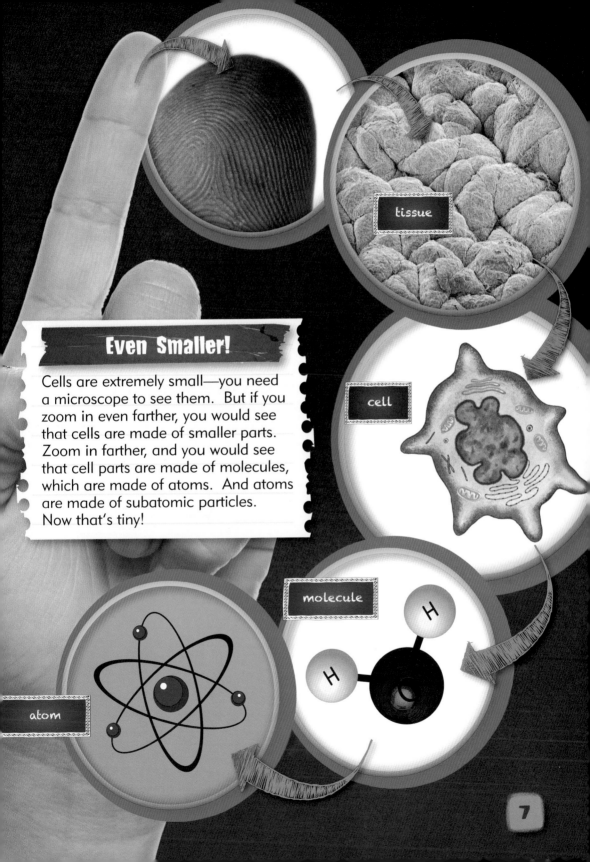

tissue

cell

Even Smaller!

Cells are extremely small—you need a microscope to see them. But if you zoom in even farther, you would see that cells are made of smaller parts. Zoom in farther, and you would see that cell parts are made of molecules, which are made of atoms. And atoms are made of subatomic particles. Now that's tiny!

molecule

atom

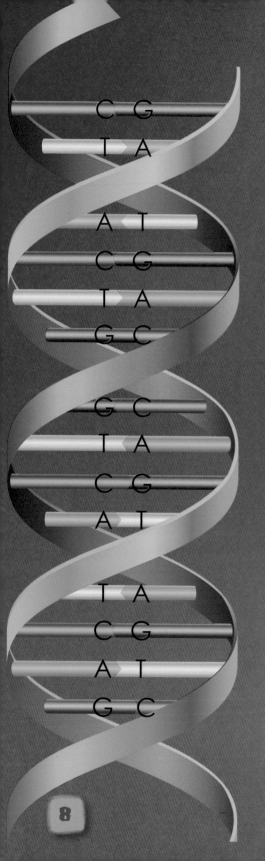

DNA Structure

DNA is too small to be seen without a very powerful microscope. But if you saw a piece, it would look a bit like a ladder. Two long strands form the sides of the ladder, and many short strands form the rungs of the ladder. But instead of being a straight ladder, DNA is a spiral staircase structure called a **double helix**.

DNA has four bases, or **nucleotides**. These nucleotides are adenine (A), thymine (T), guanine (G), and cytosine (C). The nucleotides bond together to form the rungs of the ladder. Each rung has two bases, or a base pair. A always bonds with T, and C always bonds with G. These bonded pairs contain information that the cell reads. This way, the cells know how to form and maintain the body's tissues.

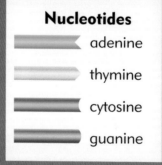

Nucleotides

adenine

thymine

cytosine

guanine

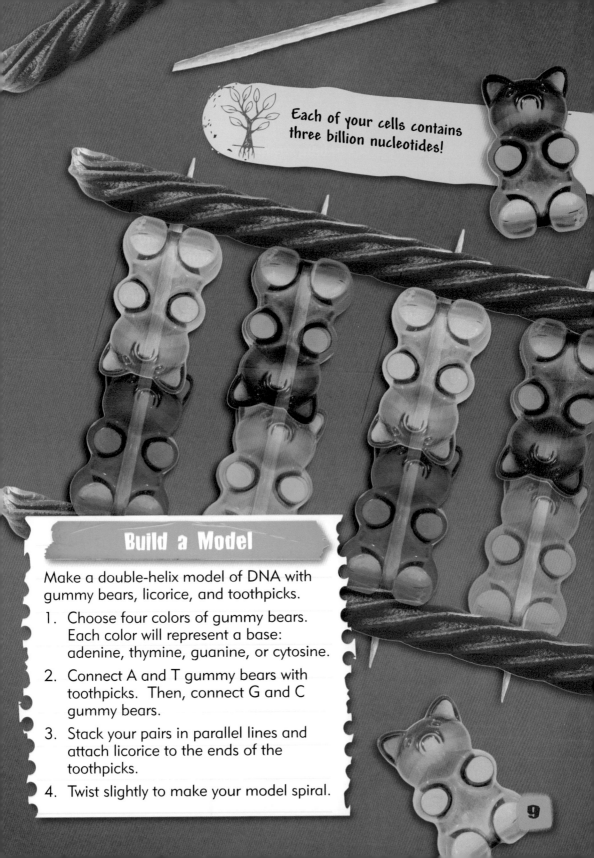

Each of your cells contains three billion nucleotides!

Build a Model

Make a double-helix model of DNA with gummy bears, licorice, and toothpicks.

1. Choose four colors of gummy bears. Each color will represent a base: adenine, thymine, guanine, or cytosine.

2. Connect A and T gummy bears with toothpicks. Then, connect G and C gummy bears.

3. Stack your pairs in parallel lines and attach licorice to the ends of the toothpicks.

4. Twist slightly to make your model spiral.

9

It's All in the Genes

Even though DNA exists in long strands, it's small sections of DNA that tell cells to make different proteins. These sections are known as genes. In all, our DNA contains about 30,000 genes. Every gene makes different proteins.

How do genes do this? The answer is easy to understand if you think of the nucleotides as letters. We all know arranging letters in various orders will create different words. (E-A-T means something different from T-E-A.) DNA records information in the same way. The nucleotides always form the same pairs on a DNA strand, but these pairs can be arranged in different orders. The order of the bases acts as a kind of code. Cells can "read" this code like a set of instructions. It gives the instructions for building proteins.

For example, the code might read T-A-A-T-C-G. Another code might read G-C-T-A-C-G. One gene codes a certain type of protein. Another gene codes a different type of protein. Our cells use this simple code to control everything they do and even how we look and act.

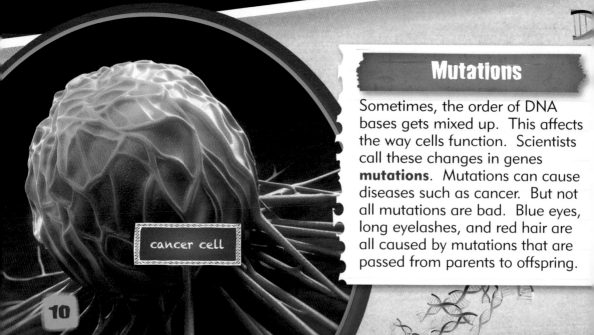

cancer cell

Mutations

Sometimes, the order of DNA bases gets mixed up. This affects the way cells function. Scientists call these changes in genes **mutations**. Mutations can cause diseases such as cancer. But not all mutations are bad. Blue eyes, long eyelashes, and red hair are all caused by mutations that are passed from parents to offspring.

DNA can make about 50,000 different kinds of proteins!

Secret Message

Four pairs of nucleotides form all the genes your body needs—just as the 26 letters of the alphabet can be used to write any book! Use the chart below to see if you can decode this secret genetic message*.

Code: ACT ATG CCG TTG AAT ATG TTG CAG AAG AGA ACA ATC CAT AGA CAG CAT CAG TTG AAG ATG ATA ATA CCA ATC AGA AAG AAA CAT ACA TTT AAA TTG AAG ACA AGT AGT TTG ATT ACT ATG ATC ACA

AAA	a	AGG	k	CCA	u
AAC	b	AGT	l	CCC	v
AAG	c	ATA	m	CCG	w
AAT	d	ATC	n	CCT	x
ACA	e	ATG	o	CGA	y
ACC	f	ATT	p	CGC	z
ACG	g	CAA	q	TTG	space
ACT	h	CAC	r	TTT	question mark
AGA	i	CAG	s		
AGC	j	CAT	t		

Have you ever wondered why some people's earlobes attach to the sides of their face and why other's wiggle freely? Have you wondered why some people have a certain hair color or why they can curl their tongue in an unusual way? The answer to these questions is genes. Your genes determine what your earlobes look like. They determine your skin color and the shape of your face.

Look at the person next to you. You share between 99.5 and 99 percent of the same genes with that person. In fact, you share 85 percent of the same genes with a zebra fish! Our differences depend on the order of the bases on the DNA strands, and a different order means a different gene.

While we might have many genes in common with others around us, our DNA most closely matches that of our families. This explains why you might have Aunt Martha's big ears or why your second toe might be longer than your big toe. Scientists study heredity to learn how genes are passed from parents to offspring. And when a trait passes on in a family, it's an inherited trait.

Smart Cell

Each cell contains DNA that stores about 1.5 gigabytes of information. That's about the amount of information that can be stored on a basic smartphone. The human body has trillions of cells. The data stored in the body is about 150 trillion gigabytes or 150 billion terabytes.

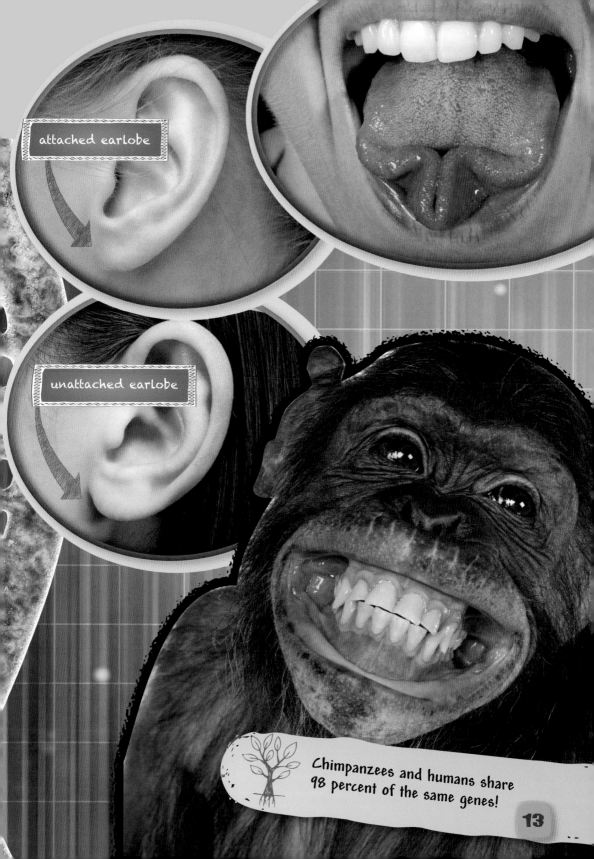

attached earlobe

unattached earlobe

Chimpanzees and humans share 98 percent of the same genes!

Organizing DNA

DNA is arranged into **chromosomes** inside a cell's nucleus. The DNA wraps around proteins like thread on a spool, creating a tight spiral. Inside a human cell, there are 23 pairs of chromosomes. Half of your chromosomes came from a cell from your mother. Half of your chromosomes came from a cell from your father. When the cells met, your first cell was formed. One chromosome from each of their pairs of chromosomes came together to make this new cell.

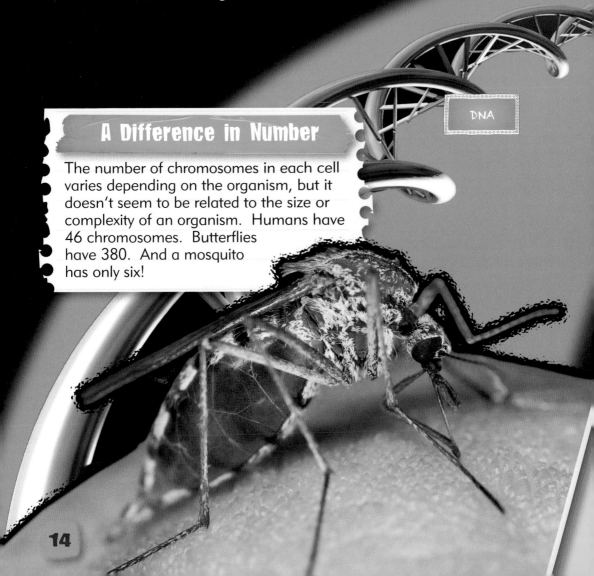

DNA

A Difference in Number

The number of chromosomes in each cell varies depending on the organism, but it doesn't seem to be related to the size or complexity of an organism. Humans have 46 chromosomes. Butterflies have 380. And a mosquito has only six!

14

cell's nucleus

chromosome

Nearly 98 percent of DNA is empty and is made up of random sequences. This is called noncoding, or "junk" DNA.

In humans, most pairs of chromosomes are the same. But there is one pair of chromosomes that determines whether a person is a boy or girl. These chromosomes are known as sex chromosomes because they determine a person's sex. A girl has two X chromosomes. A boy has one X and one Y chromosome. The mother contributes the X chromosome, but the father can give either an X or a Y sex chromosome. So, it is the father that determines whether a baby will be a boy or a girl.

You can find hundreds or even thousands of genes within a chromosome. Each chromosome in a pair has matching genes. These matching genes are found at the same location on each pair of chromosomes. But that does not mean that the genes are identical. The gene that came from your mother may be a little different from the gene that came from your father.

These different forms of the same genes, or **alleles**, provide information for the same trait. For example, certain genes determine your hair color. If your parents have different alleles for this trait, your hair color might look slightly different from that of your parents.

Sometimes, alleles make new combinations. This results in traits that are unique to only you. This happens when some alleles on the pairs of chromosomes cross over and swap places. This creates new combinations of alleles. And that can make you *you*!

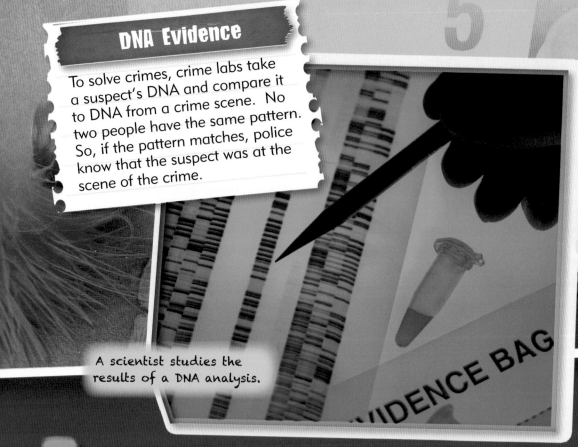

DNA Evidence

To solve crimes, crime labs take a suspect's DNA and compare it to DNA from a crime scene. No two people have the same pattern. So, if the pattern matches, police know that the suspect was at the scene of the crime.

A scientist studies the results of a DNA analysis.

poison ivy

This girl had an allergic reaction to poison ivy— she is not immune.

There is a gene that can actually make you immune to poison ivy.

Genetics

Genetics is the study of how genes control the characteristics of plants and animals. In the mid-1800s, Gregor Mendel wondered how traits were passed from generation to generation. Back then, no one knew about genes or chromosomes. He decided to study pea plants because they had simple traits. He crossbred pea plants with different-color flowers, such as purple and white, to see what the offspring would look like. He found that the first generation of flowers were all purple. But when he bred these new purple plants, sometimes a white flower was produced.

Life of Mendel

You can't take a biology class without hearing the name Mendel. But when Mendel was alive, he wasn't famous. He was a simple monk who taught science.

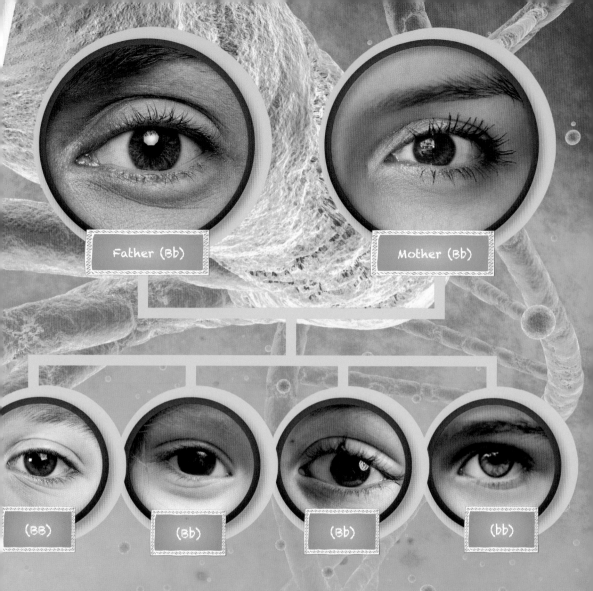

Father (Bb) Mother (Bb)

(BB) (Bb) (Bb) (bb)

Through these experiments, Mendel discovered that traits pass to offspring through pairs of genes. He found that one allele from each parent is passed to the offspring. He also found that some alleles are stronger, or more **dominant**, than the matching partner. He called the weaker alleles **recessive**. Recessive genes only appear if inherited from both parents. When a plant has two dominant alleles for color, the dominant color results. The recessive color will only appear if both parents give the offspring a recessive gene.

For example, in humans, brown eyes are dominant and blues eyes are recessive. If you have blue eyes and both your parents have brown eyes, then they must each have a recessive gene for blue eyes.

Replication

Every one of us begins as a single cell. That cell divides millions of times. The DNA in that cell copies itself so the information can pass to other cells. In this way, every cell in your body has the same DNA.

In order to make a copy, the old cells' DNA unwinds and the nucleotides separate like a zipper. There are many extra DNA bases inside the nucleus of a cell. These extra bases move toward the open strands. They connect to their base partners. Again, A and T join together, and C and G join together. This creates two identical molecules side by side.

Once DNA is copied, it wraps itself into identical sets of chromosomes. The new copies move to opposite sides of the cell, and the cell pinches in the middle. There are now two cells with the exact same DNA.

This DNA **replication** is called *mitosis*, and it is happening inside your body right now. During the past minute, millions of your cells have divided! Stomach cells, lung cells, and even the cells under your toenails are constantly replicating. The more you grow, the more cells your body will need.

Cells in your intestines live only a few days. They must constantly be replaced.

Mitosis takes place at different rates. Cells in your hair and fingernails are always dividing. Other cells, such as liver cells, only divide when injury occurs.

A cell creates a copy of itself.

Meiosis

New cells are also made by meiosis. Meiosis occurs in cells that will create new organisms.

The cell splits twice.

These half-cells combine with other half-cells to create new organisms.

Steps Forward

Mendel would be shocked to see how far genetics has come since his first experiments in the garden. In 1953, after studying the work of many scientists, Rosalind Franklin, James Watson, and Francis Crick solved the puzzle of the structure of DNA molecules. Their model made so much sense to other scientists that it was accepted right away. They were awarded a Nobel Prize for their discovery.

In 1990, a group of scientists decided they wanted to know the entire human DNA sequence. They believed that knowing this sequence could help them understand and cure genetic disorders. To do this, they created a map of human DNA. They found which genes belonged to which chromosomes. Then, they learned where each gene was located on each chromosome. Finally, they learned the order of DNA bases. It took them 13 years to map the entire human **genome**.

Scientists hope to use this information in the future to help people. They might be able to select just the right medicine to treat a person's ailments based on his or her DNA. Or they might be able to turn off the genes that contribute to certain diseases, such as obesity. They might even be able to prevent cancer growth in some patients.

The word *genome* comes from combining two words: *gene* and *chromosome*.

1865—Gregor Mendel completes pea plant experiment.

1869—Friedrich Miescher discovers DNA and calls it nuclein.

1953—Rosalind Franklin, James Watson, and Francis Crick discover that DNA has a double helix.

1990—The Human Genome Project begins.

1996—Dolly the sheep is cloned.

1999—Human chromosome (chromosome 22) is decoded.

2003—The Human Genome Project is completed.

Scientists have also been learning about changing the genes of living creatures. They have been experimenting with **cloning**. They're testing ways to copy the DNA of one creature and produce a clone with the exact DNA of the original animal.

In 1996, scientists produced the first living cloned mammal. She was a sheep named Dolly. To do this, they took the DNA from a cell in an adult sheep. It took 275 tries to create Dolly. She grew up and even produced four offspring. But after seven years, Dolly showed signs of disease found only in sheep twice her age. She died six years later.

The cloning of Dolly has sparked debates. It makes some people worry about using science to clone humans. They wonder if cloning might be immoral or will produce health problems in the clones. But some other people disagree. They say that human cloning can be used to cure diseases. Some scientists are working to clone organs for this purpose. This means that if you need a new heart, scientists could use your DNA to make you a new heart.

In 2001, the first cat was cloned. Her name, CC, stands for Copy Cat. It took 188 tries to successfully make CC.

Dolly

Bioprinting

Using advanced computer programs, scientists are able to enter a design for a body part and then layer cells to create it. They are able to create kidneys, ears, skin, bones, and blood cells. It is called *bioprinting*.

bioprinter

bioartificial tissue

Cloning in Nature

Some animals, such as certain types of amphibians, reptiles, and insects, produce offspring that are the clone of the mother's eggs. This occurs when offspring develop from unfertilized eggs. It is called *parthenogenesis*.

Whiptail lizards can produce offspring through parthenogenesis.

Looking Ahead

It's strange to think that you share some of your DNA with your parents and grandparents. Stranger still to think that you share some with your great-great-great-great-great-great grandmother, too! In this way, we are living pieces of those who came before us. If you have children one day, you will pass this legacy on to them.

DNA has been around for millions of years, and still its message is loud and clear. It's written in code in every cell of every living thing. The code is so simple that it allows for endless possibilities. We have come a long way in our quest to understand ourselves through genetics. But there is still so much more to be discovered. The future of DNA discoveries is exciting. Scientists hope to use their knowledge of DNA to cure diseases and improve our lives. But with every answer we find, new questions arise. Who knows what challenges await future scientists?

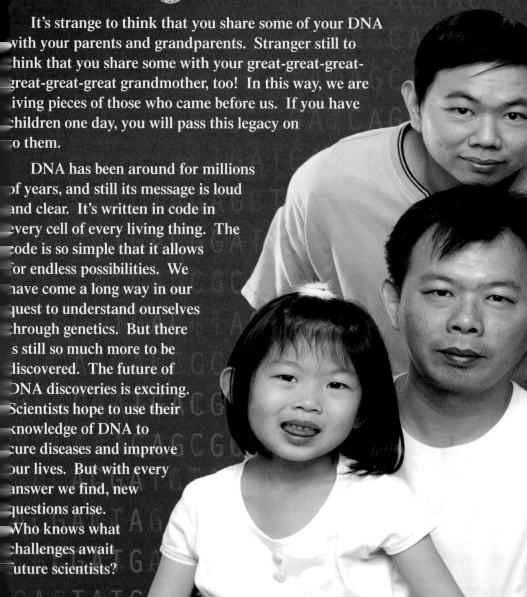

"The pace of discovery is going unbelievably fast."
—James D. Watson

Think Like a Scientist

How can you examine DNA? Experiment and find out!

What to Get

- $\frac{1}{2}$ cup water
- $\frac{1}{2}$ cup rubbing alcohol
- 1 teaspoon salt
- 2 plastic cups
- 2 strawberries (fresh or frozen)
- 2 tsp. dish soap

- coffee filter
- craft stick
- measuring cup
- measuring spoon
- plastic zipper bag

What to Do

1 Remove leaves or stems from the strawberries. Place strawberries in the zipper bag and mash them until they are completely crushed.

2 Mix the dish soap, salt, and water in a plastic cup with the craft stick. Pour the mixture into the bag and gently mash it together.

3 Place the coffee filter over the second plastic cup and pour the mixture through the filter. Gently squeeze the filter to get as much liquid into the cup as possible.

4 Add the rubbing alcohol to the same cup. Do not stir.

5 Use the craft stick to pick up the white, cloudy mixture. What do you observe? What do you think this mixture is?

Glossary

alleles—slightly different forms of the same gene that determine genetic traits

chromosomes—parts of cells that contain genes that control how living things grow

cloning—growing a cell that has exactly the same genes as one other organism

deoxyribonucleic acid—substance that carries genetic information in the cells of living things

dominant—will always cause a particular characteristic to show

double helix—the shape formed by two parallel lines that twist around each other

genes—parts of cells that control or influence the appearance and growth of living things

genetics—the scientific study of how genes control the characteristics of living things

genome—all of the genes and genetic information within an organism

heredity—the process by which characteristics are passed from parents to offspring through the parents' genes

inherited—to have a characteristic because of the genes that you get from your parents when you are born

molecules—the smallest possible amounts of particular substances that have all the characteristics of those substances

mutations—changes in chromosomes or genes that result in new traits

nucleotides—the four bases on a DNA strand

proteins—large molecules that help cells function

recessive—causing or relating to a characteristic or condition that the offspring will have only if both its parents have it

replication—the act of copying something exactly

trait—a quality that makes one living thing different from another

Index

Nature or Nurture?

Write all the traits that describe you, including what you look like and what you like to do. What traits or characteristics cannot be seen in a photograph or mirror? Do you think these traits are a result of your DNA or the environment you grew up in?